THE GRINDR SERIAL KILLER

THE GRINDR SERIAL KILLER

THE TRUE STORY OF STEPHEN PORT

ALAN R. WARREN

COPYRIGHT

THE GRINDR SERIAL KILLER: The True Story of Stephen Port
Written by Alan R. Warren

Published in Canada

Copyright @ 2020 by Alan R. Warren

All rights reserved. No part of this book may be reproduced, scanned, or distributed in any printed or electronic form without permission of the author. The unauthorized reproduction of a copyrighted work is illegal. Criminal copyright infringement, including infringement without monetary gain, is investigated by the FBI and is punishable by fines and federal imprisonment. Please do not participate in or encourage privacy of copyrighted materials in violation of the author's rights. Purchase only authorized editions.

This is a work of nonfiction. No names have been changed, no characters invented, no events fabricated.

Cover design, formatting, layout, and editing by Evening Sky Publishing Services

BOOK DESCRIPTION

In today's world where meeting people for the purpose of having sex with a simple click on your phone, a new type of gay sex called "party n play" or "Chemsex" has become all the rage in the mainstream.

Several young gay men were being found dead appearing to have overdosed on the favorite sex drugs used at these Chemsex parties, in a city church yard in east London. Was this what the metro police claimed it was "a sex drug overdose" or was there something more going on here?

It would soon be discovered that a popular 41-year-old, Stephen Port, who had appeared on *Celebrity Chef UK* would be arrested and charged with four of the young men's murders by overdosing them with GBH (the Date Rape Drug), enough to kill the men, and then raping them and leaving their bodies out in a church yard.

Since the conviction of "Celebrity Chef UK," Stephen Port, the police are now reviewing 58 other mysterious deaths by overdose where the body was found dead in the same area of London. There are now 17 police officers under investigation for not investigating the crimes because of their homophobia.

Included are several of the personal letters convicted serial killer Stephen Port sent to his friend and pen-pal Cody Lachey which reveals what he claims happened to each of the victims and what really happened in these Chemsex parties. You will also find out some of Port's personal details that you wouldn't expect to hear.

INTRODUCTION

It was a crisp cloudy fall day on Thursday October 15, 2015 when the London Metropolitan Police came to Stephen Port's one-bedroom flat on Cooke Street in Barking, East London, to place Port into custody and charge him with the murders of four men. The police also charged Port with six counts of administering a poison, seven charges of rape and four charges of sexual assault. It would be while Port was in custody in July of 2016, that the prosecutors added another eight counts of poisoning for a total of twenty-nine charges against him.

When Stephen Port was arrested, he placed into the Level an HMP (Her Majesties Prison) Belmarsh, which is the highest security prison category based on the severity of the crime, as well as the risk posed if the prisoner would escape. The prison is located adjacent to the Woolwich Crown Court, in South-East London, where quite often the high-profile cases are heard. The Belmarsh Prison was also used to house all people who posed a threat to the National Security of the country, quite a few of them were detained indefinitely without charge under the Crime and Security Act of 2001.

According to a report by *The Daily Mail* in the U.K. from May 17, 2016, "the Belmarsh maximum security jail is like a jihadist training camp, where extremists brainwash young prisoners to spread the terror message across the whole prison system," a former inmate claimed in the report. A group of jihadists who call themselves "The Akhi" (Arabic for brother) appear to almost run the prison. At the time of this report there were 28 inmates being held for terrorist related offenses.

This creates a problem for the other inmates that are being held in the prison, especially young offenders like Stephen Port, who the Akhi try to indoctrinate and brainwash into their beliefs and create a larger network of terrorists in the prison. Someone like Port also has the problems of his sexuality, as it would not be accepted in such an extreme group as the Akhi, could also become a threat to his own life.

It was this type of atmosphere that existed in the Belmarsh Prison that would leave Stephen Port very alone and feeling quite vulnerable. His parents were not able to visit Stephen and he would be in his cell for up to 23 hours per day, where his only means of communication would be to exchange letters with his family, friends or anybody on the outside. This is where a man by the name of Cody Lachey would come into Stephen's life to help fill the empty void that Stephen had been now living locked away in prison.

It would have been in the winter of 2015 when Stephen would receive a letter in prison from someone he had never heard of before. It wouldn't be long before

Stephen realized that being all over the news on television, radio and the internet would put him in the spotlight, not only in the prison, but in the UK and the World. Soon he would start getting letters from dozens of both men and women looking to get to know him, quite often in a romantic way.

I met Cody Lachey after seeing him on a documentary called *Crime and Investigation*. Cody had been on the program which discussed several serial killers in Britain, and he had not only known some of them, but also communicated with them, and one of them was Stephen Port.

Cody Lachey was an ex-convict who had been in prison in the UK three times, once in the HMP Manchester known as the "Notorious Strangeways" and twice in Salford's Forest Bank Prison. Cody had been involved in the criminal underworld and a drug dealer. The 35-year-old, 6"4" had been shot at and stabbed several times before serving his time in prison.

Cody now is reformed and living in Manchester, England, where he has become a crime commentator which covers all aspects of his own personal history of living the life of crime and being in prisons. He has been on several documentaries, spoke to criminology students, and given in depth perspectives on prison reform in the UK. Cody told me,

---

"It was from my childhood where I was raised watching serial killer, and gangster documentaries that I went on to be involved with all of the lifestyle. My early lifestyle is also what started me

> on writing to serial killers who were in prison. I really enjoyed discussing the cases with he killers and wanted to hear their sides of the story.
>
> I first wrote to Stephen Port after he was charged with the four murders and a whole host of other offences. I read a news article that stated that Port was in the HMP Belmarsh, and I knew how to write to prisoners from being in prison myself earlier. So, I wrote to him and he replied, and we went from there.
>
> We corresponded for months and I couldn't believe how open he was discussing his case with me from the very first letter. As a former prisoner myself it was obvious that he wasn't clued up that he was on remand, and it was well known that if you're in prison on remand you don't discuss your case with anyone whether that be speaking on the phone or in letters. Even with your cell-mate you say nothing, as anything you say or do can be used as evidence against you, but Port was very much an open book."

I have included some of the most important of these letters in this book. They will give you the reader a great perspective on who Stephen Port is and how he thinks. Stephen describes what happened on the nights of each one of these crimes and offers his defense to the murders. Did Stephen Port kill these men and possibly more, or was he just an innocent man who got himself into a lifestyle of Chemsex, where it was just bad luck that at least four of his partners who participated in Chemsex with him, turned up dead?

As with many of my other true crime books before this one, there is also a question of how the police and courts dealt with these crimes based on the status and circumstances of the victims. Even if law enforcement didn't care that each of the murder victims were gay, there is still a question of why law enforcement did not do anything to investigate each one of these crimes. As you read through the cases of each one of these murder victims, and see that there was absolutely no investigation done, even when the autopsies showed us that there were definite questions, the metro police just closed each case and ruled them overdoses.

This is a story of a serial killer, and how he was aided by the unfortunate uncaring attitude of the metropolitan police that ignored a mountain of evidence suggesting that there were several murders of the gay community going on in Barking, but because of their uncaring attitude, decided not to bother to investigate. This left a serial killer a free reign to do what he wanted to, when he wanted to and even how he wanted to do it.

The police are now reassessing 58 unexplained deaths of homosexuals involving the date rape drug GHB, that occurred between June of 2011 and October 2015, to make sure that foul play has not been missed. It should be mentioned that the churchyard at St. Margaret was known as a place for men to meet each other for quick anonymous sexual encounters, this was one of the reasons that the police never thought twice about a gay man being found dead on the grounds from an overdose.

1

LET ME SHOW YOU THE WORLD IN MY EYES

It was on February 22 in 1975 when Stephen John Port was born in Southend-On-Sea, in Britain. His parents moved to Dagenham about one year after he was born. At school Stephen spent most of his time alone and very withdrawn, not really getting along with the other students. His neighbors always considered Stephen as a much older soul, almost like an adult, and not a child. This is probably why he didn't socialize with the other students at school much.

Stephen had one sister, Sharon, who was 2 years older than him, and his parents Albert and Joan Port. The parents were not comfortable with Stephen's lifestyle of being gay, but they tolerated it. Stephen's father, Albert, blamed Stephen's lifestyle on the fact that he was shy and an introvert. In Albert's mind, this had led someone to take advantage of Stephen and turn him gay. Albert also didn't like the fact that his son would never listen to any of his advice.

Joan Port was closer to Stephen and would regularly

visit him at his apartment. She said that Stephen was very neat and tidy, always keeping his apartment clean and in order. Sharon, Stephen's sister also stated that there was a man that always paid for Stephen's household bills on a regular basis, but she had never met the man and didn't know who he was.

Stephen Port claimed to have worked as an expert special needs teacher at Westminster Kingsway College, in King's Cross and was also a former Seaman at the Royal Navy. His resume also claimed that he had graduated from the University of Oxford and was from Hornchurch in Barking, East London.

Stephen had all this information on his Facebook page as well as saying that he had worked as a chef and helped disabled students learn how to cook. Before that, it claimed that he was a door to door sales clerk.

Link to Stephen Port's Facebook Page

When talking to Stephen's parents, they stated that Stephen was a special needs teacher and that he had also worked as a chef. They denied that Stephen had ever gone to Oxford University.

Although Stephen claimed to have done all of these jobs listed on his resume and Facebook page, he was really a male escort and worked as a cook at a bus stop café. He started selling his body to men when he was about 30 years-old where he charged 800 pounds per night or 100 pounds per 1-hour session. Stephen was very popular with his escort services and had several great reviews on *The Daily Mail*.

LET ME SHOW YOU THE WORLD IN MY EYES | 3

| Stephen Port

I HOPE I'M OLD BEFORE I DIE ...

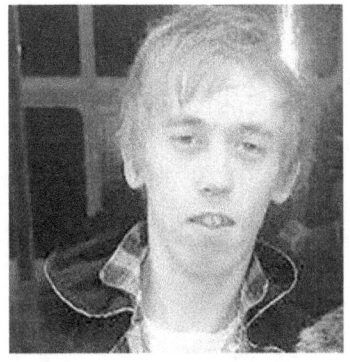

Anthony Patrick Walgate

Anthony Patrick Walgate, 23, was a second-year design, fashion, and art student at the University of Middlesex. When Anthony had moved from Hull to attend the University for design, it caused him a severe financial hardship, so Anthony had placed an ad on the *Sleepy Boys* app as a male escort and began earning extra cash to help support himself during college.

On June 17, 2014, Stephen Port contacted Anthony on

Sleepy Boys and had offered Anthony 800 GBP to come to Stephen's home overnight for sex. After Walgate set up the appointment and location with Port, he told his friend about the date and where he would be going, and even the fake name of his client "Jo Dean," just in case as Anthony said, "I get killed."

Right after Port booked the appointment with Anthony, he went online and searched for drug rape pornography. Port then went to the Barking rail station at 10 p.m. to meet Walgate and bring him back to his flat.

Early the morning of June 19, 2014, the police received a phone call about a dead body being found in front of an apartment building on Cooke Street.

---

999 Dispatcher: "Emergency ambulance, what's the address of the emergency?"

Caller: I think it's Cooke Street. There's a young boy. I think he's collapsed outside, I don't know."

Dispatcher: "Outside of which number?"

Caller: "um 47 or 58."

Dispatcher: "Sorry?"

Caller: "47 or 58."

Dispatcher: "47 Cooke Street."

Caller: "Yeah."

Dispatcher: "Right, What area?"

Caller: "Barking. Looks like he's collapsed or had a seizure or something, or he's just drunk."

Dispatcher: "Ok, what's the telephone number you are calling from?"

Caller: "I'll go get my car."

Dispatcher: "Alright, don't worry about that. What's the telephone number you are calling from?"

Stephen Port puts the phone down and goes quiet.
Dispatcher: "Hello!?"
The 999 dispatcher calls Stephen Port back,

Dispatcher: "Hello, it's the ambulance service, we were cut off there. Could you confirm your location?"

Caller: "Ahh I've just driven away now."

Dispatcher: "Where was the fella outside of?"

Caller: "Uh Cooke Street."

Dispatcher: "What number?"

Caller: "um I don't know, I didn't look."

Dispatcher: "You said 47 before?"

Caller: "Yeah I did 47, yeah."

Dispatcher: "So you think they had a seizure, is that correct?"

Caller: "umm uh yeah, yep."

Dispatcher: "So you were passing by in your car?"

Caller: "Yes."

Dispatcher: "Ok, and you've drove past now, so you're no longer there?"

Caller: "That's right."

Dispatcher: "How old did he look to you sir?"

Caller: "Twenties."

Dispatcher: "Do you know if he was awake?"

Caller: "No."

Dispatcher: "Do you know if he was breathing?"

Caller: "No, I don't know."

Dispatcher: "Did you see anything happen at all?"

Caller: "No."

Dispatcher: "No, you just think he may have possibly had a seizure, and he was lying there on the floor?"

Caller: "Yes."

Dispatcher: "Ok, thanks for letting us know, we'll get someone there as soon as we can."

Caller: "Okay."

Dispatcher: "Thank you."

The caller hangs up on the dispatcher again, so the 999 dispatcher calls him back.

Dispatcher: "Hello Sir. It's the ambulance service, sorry to bother you again, it was definitely Cooke street, that the patient was on?"

Caller: "Yes, definitely, I passed him and it was Cooke Street."

Dispatcher: "Ok, and were you just kinda driving passed, and just saw the patient lying there?"

Caller: "I was just driving out of my car park."

Dispatcher: "Is your car park there?"

Caller: "and I saw him lying on the floor."

Dispatcher: "okay."

Caller: "I got out, had a look at him."

Dispatcher: "yes."

Caller: "Called you and got back into my car."

Dispatcher: "Alright, no worries, no worries, just wanted to be sure. Thank you for your help, sir and sorry to bother you again."

Caller: "Okay no worries."

Dispatcher: "Bye bye."

When the police arrived at the scene, they found the body of Anthony Walgate sitting with his back leaned against the apartment building wall. His shirt had been pulled up and rested around his chest and the zipper in his pants had been left opened. His head was facing downwards as if he was sleeping.

The police also found that Anthony's underwear had been removed and put back on but inside out. He was bruised in 14 places throughout the body and had died from an overdose of the drug GHB. There was a bottle of the GHB drug found in the dead man's pocket. After police inquiry was completed, they ruled that the death was not homicide or a sex crime, but a drug overdose.

The police investigated the number they received the report of the collapsed man from, and they found out the phone belonged to Stephen Port. A week after the body was discovered the officers went to ask Port some questions about how he had found the body.

It was after a small investigation that the police found out that Stephen Port had hired Walgate as a male escort, so they arrested Port for suspicion of perverting the course of justice. In simple terms basically, Port was charged with lying to the police.

During Port's trial for lying to the police, he admitted that he had Walgate in his apartment for sex, and that Walgate took the GHB willingly. Port claimed,

> "When I met Mr. Walgate for sex, the young man had wanted to have some stuff to make him horny and high. I saw that he had a little brown bottle with him."

It wasn't until after Port returned from a night shift at the bus stop diner that he found Walgate stiff and rigid in his bed, making a gurgling noise. Port then panicked and dragged the body out of his apartment building and placed him against the wall outside. Port did not check to see if Anthony was still alive. He just got into his car and started to drive, and that's when he decided to call the 999-ambulance service.

The jury heard that in a police interview that day, Mr. Port asked a detective:

> "Can I just say for the scenario - if it was an accident, and if he did have a fit in my place, is that still my fault?"

Initially, Mr. Rees said, the defendant denied having met Mr. Walgate but later admitted spending time in his flat with him, where Mr. Port claimed Mr. Walgate willingly took GHB/GBL.

Port was found guilty and given 8 months in jail as a sentence, but only served 3 months before being released, but with an electronic tag to be placed on his leg until June of 2015. The police then closed the case.

Kate Whelan, Anthony Walgate's aunt, made an emotional appeal for people to take care using dating websites and apps.

> "It was four years ago that Ant was murdered by a predatory serial sex fiend. Age just 23 our Ant was enjoying university and had an exciting future. Our lives will never be the same. We live daily with trauma, shock, anger and pain. Please be careful if you are using dating apps. Although your kids are young adults and you feel they are sensible please reinforce the stranger danger warnings. The internet is a fabulous thing but be aware there are predators."

3

PLEASE GOD, NOT ANOTHER ONE

Barking is a small town located in East London, in the United Kingdom, with a population of about 187,000 people, that was primarily a fishing and farming community. The name of Barking came from the English slang for "Barking Mad" which has been attributed to the alleged insane asylum that was attached to the Barking Abbey that was part of the St. Margaret's Church dating back to the 13th century.

On August 20, 2014, the summer was winding down and East London resident Barbra Denham, 67, leashed her border collie named Max, to take him for his daily walk. She would always take much the same route which through the quiet and grassy property of the St. Catherine's Church. It was really the perfect place to walk as she could unleash her dog and not worry about car traffic or a lot of people around. This was something she had done for the 28 years that she had lived in the area, only this time things would be different.

When Barbara entered the Church grounds things were normal, the sky was dark and gray, the grass was damp from the rain that fell earlier that morning. She unleashed Max to let him run free and do his business as he always had done. She started to walk slowly towards the church and always admired the architecture and thought about how amazing it would have been to live in such an impressive building or castle. As she got towards the Abbey on the Church grounds, she noticed a young man sitting upright with his back against the stone wall. Barbara thought she would approach the man and say hi, but as she got up close enough to talk with him, she noticed that he didn't seem to be moving. Barbara claimed,

---

"I saw what I thought was a man sitting down on the grass, with his head slightly down, and his back against the wall. He was wearing dark glasses slanted over his face and although I have seen a lot of homeless people sleeping in the area, I just knew something wasn't right."

It was then that Barbara started to clap her hands real loud and shout out "WooHoo." There was no response or movement from the young man.

"He has a bluish pallor and when I saw his eyes glassed over, I knew he was dead. There was no blood, he looked very peaceful."

Ms. Denham said that she remained calm when she realized that she had found a dead body.

"I don't know whether it is watching horror programs or murder mysteries, but I was quite calm. I took out my phone and called the emergency services and they came quite quickly."

It was two days later that her local paper announced that the young man she had found in the park, only 21, had died in a drug overdose. This was in East London, and the area was known for a lot of drug use and petty crime, so though it was a big shock to have found a dead body in the park, it wasn't a total surprise for there to have been a drug overdose in the area.

Three weeks later, in September, Barbara was out walking her collie Max again in the same park, when she noticed another young man sitting in the exact same place that she had found the dead body in August.

"This man was sitting the exact same way, with his head face down as if he was sleeping too."

Right away Barbra thought to herself,

"Please God, no, not another one. Please let him be a boy who is just drunk or something. I suppose I knew before I went over that he was dead, I just knew. But I touched his ankle where his skin was exposed and felt it was cold."

She took her cell phone from her purse and called the police,

---

"I'm the lady that found the first body, I have found another young boy."

Barbara said with a shakiness in her voice,

"To have found two young men in the same position, it did upset me. I was a bit concerned over my reaction really because I was trying to keep control of myself. I really did feel sorry for both, for the families. A third body was found on the other side of the wall by someone else, I don't know how soon after the second one that I found. It was luck I didn't find that one as well."

The first body was identified as Gabriel Kovari, 22, and recently moved to London from Slovakia. The second was Daniel Whitworth, 21, from Gravesend in Kent who worked as a chef. Not only had both men been found dead in the exact same place in the exact same park, but the second body, Whitworth had a suicide note placed beside him in the park. The note suggested that he was responsible for the death of the first body found (Kovari) by overdosing on the party drug GHB during a sexual encounter they had, and therefore Whitworth committed suicide as he could not deal with the guilt.

When the parents of Daniel Whitworth were shown the note that was supposedly written by Daniel and they both said that it was not written by their son. They said the response of the police was "it is what it is, and you just have to deal with it."

Gabriel Kovari, 22, who was originally from Slovakia left his home because he felt the people there were too conservative and intolerant. When he got to London, he found a job at a little shop and in August met Port, who invited Gabriel to stay on his couch until he got on his feet. Port always called Gabriel "My Slovakian Twink flat mate." Gabriel was left on the church grounds wearing sunglasses and his suitcase with his belongings and some papers.

Gabriel's mother, a pharmacist, described Gabriel as a gifted artist who wanted to make a difference.

> "He was full of love and care for others and loved the company of his friends, he was very inquisitive and special child, gifted in arts."

After Gabriel was found dead, Port friended Gabriel's Spanish boyfriend Thierry Amondo on Facebook pretending to be an American student in London by the name of Jon Luck. He did this so that he could keep tabs on if the police told of any suspects and who they were.

During the police interview in 2015, Port denied any involvement,

---

> "I don't give anybody drugs, whenever he went to parties Daniel would give everyone the drugs."

Daniel Whitworth was the second body found. He had a suicide note in his left hand. The suicide note claimed that it was because he (Daniel) blamed himself for the death of Gabriel Kovari (the first dead body found by the dog walker in the churchyard) by an overdose during sex. The police took the note at face-value and no attempt was made to further investigate his death.

Daniel Whitworth was from Gravesend, Kent. Whitworth's step-mother says that when police informed her of his death, they led her to believe he had overdosed on drugs, despite no investigation having taken place, and discounted the bruising under his arms. A coroner later stated that third-party involvement could not be ruled out.

Suicide note found on the body of Daniel Whitworth

SUICIDE NOTE TRANSCRIPTION

"I am sorry to everyone, mainly my family, but I can't go on anymore. I took the life of my friend Gabriel Kline, we was just having some fun at a mate's place and I got carried away and gave him another shot of G. I didn't notice while we was having sex that he had stopped breathing. I tried everything to get him to breathe again but it was too late. It was an accident, but I blame myself for what happened, and I didn't tell my family I went out. I know I would go to prison if I go to the police and I can't do that to my family and at least this way I can at least be with Gabriel again, I hope he will forgive me.

BTW Please do not blame the guy I was with last night, we only had sex then I left, he knows nothing of what I have done. I have taken what G I have left with sleeping pills so if it does kill me it's what I deserve. Feeling dizey (misspelled on purpose) now as I took 10 minutes ago so hoping you understand my writing. I dropped my phone on my way here so it should be in grass somewhere. Sorry to everyone." Love always, Daniel P.W.

They took the supposed suicide note left with his body at face value, sending a small fragment to her and Whitworth's father, asking them to verify whether it was his handwriting. Although it was established by both of Whitworth's parents that the handwriting on the note was not that of their sons, Dagenham Police recorded this as confirmation it was Whitworth's handwriting. The police had not submitted the note for expert analysis.

When the couple were later shown the complete document, Whitworth's father immediately commented that he saw nothing to indicate it had been written by his son. The couple had also asked whether the police had investigated who was meant by, "the guy I was with last night," and that the response was that it would never be possible to find out all the answers. Asking about challenging the open verdict or continuing the investigation, his stepmother encountered what she described as an attitude of,

---

"It is what it is, deal with it."

Daniel Whitworth

4

MURDER OF JACK TAYLOR

Jack Taylor

These first three victims were initially thought not to have died in suspicious circumstances, and despite even the local police force's LGBT advisory group reporting that there was a serial killer at large, the police told the families of the victims and the public that the crimes were not linked.

Jack Taylor was a 25-year-old fork-lift operator from

Hull and was out with friends partying at a gay night club in the area until about 10 p.m. on the night of Friday September 13. Like a lot of people today, they were out socializing and using their cell phone apps at the same time. This was when Jack met Stephen on the gay hook up app called *Grindr*. They chatted for a little while and one thing that Stephen had asked Jack became relevant in the future court case. "Do you take tea," which was a street name for crystal meth. Jack answered no that he had never done it, and they decided to meet up at the Barking Rail Station.

After they met, Stephen walked back to his one-bedroom apartment, where it was thought he had spiked Jack's drink with GHB. After Jack passed out, he injected Jack with poppers and raped him. Jack's body was left at the St. Margaret's church leaning against the same fence as the two previous bodies were, only on the opposite side.

When the police arrived, they found Jack leaned up against the brick fence, as the two other bodies had been. His shirt had been pulled up and rested around his chest, as if he was dragged to where he laid.

On the body they found a syringe that had not been used, and a small container that held two little bottles. After an inquiry again, the police ruled that Jack had died of an overdose, but it had been self-inflicted and there was no connection with the victim's death and the other bodies that had been found at the park earlier. The death was treated as non-suspicious.

Jack's two sisters, Jenny and Donna Taylor, both knew that their brother never used drugs, and thought that him overdosing wasn't right. Even weirder was the idea that Jack was supposed to have overdosed by shooting up, but the needle found on him had never been used. The sisters were also not understanding why the police did not test any of the evidence for DNA or try to find out what Jack was doing in that area of town since he didn't live there.

After getting no help from the police, except to hear that their brother's death was an overdose and it was not connected to any other body that had been found in the park, the sisters decided to get their own investigator to try and find out what happened to their brother.

Taylor's sister reported the police simply telling the family, "Jack's dead," and accepting the syringe in his pocket, white powder in his wallet and needle marks on his arm as proof that he had sat down by himself and overdosed on drugs. They would not listen to the fact that their brother was very anti-drugs.

Jack's sisters contacted Barking Dagenham Police 11 days after his death for an update on their investigation, and were astonished to discover that none was taking place. Their own research alerted them to the three previous cases. The police responded by denying there was any connection.

Eventually, two weeks after his death, the police agreed to take the two sisters to where Taylor's body had been found, and at Barking Station told them that CCTV footage of Taylor and another man had been found. The sisters were surprised not to have been notified, and more surprised to be told the police were not attempting to identify the other man.

One described the attitude of the police as "shocking." In response to their questioning the credibility of the police account of what the footage showed, a sergeant later contacted them to say that upon review, the footage did not show Taylor entering the churchyard alone. They then requested that images of the other man be made public in order to identify him; the police were reluctant, saying that they did not normally release CCTV images, but eventually gave in, and two days later Port was identified from the images and arrested

Donna Taylor, Jack's mother, said that the police should be held accountable for their son's death. She has accused the police of "class, gender, and sexual bias" and has suggested that lives may have been saved had they acted sooner.

After each of the four bodies were examined by the forensic psychologist, Nadia Persaud, the inquest returned an open verdict. An open verdict means that there needs to be more questions answered for them to conclude for the reason for the deaths.

Nadia went on to say,

"The most concerning are the findings by the pathologist of manual handling prior to the deaths. There was a bed sheet that one of the bodies was wrapped in, sunglasses on another bodies face, and bottles of GHB on or near to, all four of the bodies, and none of them were tested for fingerprints or DNA."

INTERROGATION OF STEPHEN PORT

Stephen Port was finally brought in and interrogated by police on October 15, 2015.

POLICE INTERVIEWER: "So did you have any involvement in death of the male that we spoke about just a short while ago, Gabrielle Guevara or Gabrielle Kline?"

STEPHEN PORT: "No I did not, no."

PI: "Were you involved in administering any drugs or poison or noxious substances to him?"

SP: "No I don't administer drugs to anyone or give drugs to anyone. Um that's done at the party by someone, of the name organized."

PI: "Who is that, sorry?"

SP: "Daniel. He organized it. Sometimes he the dude that hands out the drugs to the guests."

PI: "Daniel?"

SP: "Yeah."

The detective moved a picture across the table face up towards Port.

> PI: "Daniel. This is the man that you spoke of earlier?"
>
> SP: "I don't know. I mean it might be the same guy, I don't know, but he's the only Daniel I know."

There was a short pause as Port continued to look down at the papers that the detective had placed in front of him.

> SP: "Like he does what I did, he'd pick up guys and bring them to the party."
>
> PI: "Yes."
>
> SP: "But he would stay longer and would administer drugs, hand out drugs, or whatever, but I would leave, and he would stay."
>
> PI: "And did you go with Daniel to meet people?"
>
> SP: "No, No. I knew he was doing the same as I was, but I would see him at the party and I had a brief conversation about it, but I never actually engaged with him outside of that."
>
> PI: "Outside of the party?"

> SP: "That's right."
> PI: "Which parties were these?"
> SP: "All sorts, Frat parties."
> PI: "Frat parties."

Another pause in the conversation occurred until Port covered him mouth and coughed a few times.

> PI: "So when was the first occasion that you met the person that you are talking of the man you know as Daniel?"
>
> SP: "It was on the first few occasions I was there, with Rafa Scott, Daniel was there. I don't even know if it's the same Daniel that we are even talking about. He is the only Daniel I can recall as such, he's the only one that rings a bell."
>
> PI: "You think his name was Whitford?"
>
> SP: "He was tall, almost as tall as me, brown hair."
>
> PI: "It might help you if I showed you a picture. We call this CRT.

The investigator started to direct Port's attention to the pictures that he had placed on the table in front of him.

> PI: "You see this is Jack Taylor."

Port slid the picture of Jack Taylor over towards himself and took a long quiet stare at it.

SP: "I don't pay full attention to the guys faces when I have been to the parties, but I don't recognize his face."

PI: "So you don't recognize his face?"

SP: "No I do not, no."

PI: "That's Jack Taylor, so you don't recognize Jack Taylor?"

SP: "No, I do not."

PI: "So, have you ever slept with this man?"

SP: "No."

PI: "Or had sexual intercourse with him?"

SP: "He doesn't look like the type I would go for myself."

PI: "He's not the sort of person you would go for?"

SP: "No, I don't want, he's more yoga drinking boys, and he looks older. He doesn't look like some of the boys I've taken to parties, he's not one of them."

PI: "So you don't recognize him as being one of them?"

SP: "No."

PI: "No? Okay."

The detective then picked up the picture of Jack Taylor and started to put it away amongst the other papers and pictures that he had on the table.

PI: "Again Jack was found dead on the 14th of September 2015. Stephen did you have any involvement in his death?"

SP: "I did not, no…no."

PI: "Did you kill Jack Taylor?"

SP: "I did not, no…. no."

PI: "Did you administer any drugs or noxious substances to him?"

SP: "No no."

PI: "With the intention of causing him harm?"

SP: "no….no, I did not, no."

PI: "And you say you've never seen him before, is that right?"

SP: "That's right."

PI: "That's right."

The detective left the room for a short break. When he returned this time, he had what looked like several maps with him. He sat down and started placing the maps around the table.

PI: "What I've got right here is several maps, it's not easy to get it all in one piece of paper. Just so were clear here, again it shows your home address and it shows you the church, St. Margaret's and then behind it you've got the Abbey and the primary school. The walls around the Abbey, have you ever had any reason to go into that area?"

SP: "No."

PI: "Have you ever been through into the Abbey?"

SP: "Ahh, no I haven't, no. Those are touchy areas. I once went to the church with my ex Danny on Christmas day, went to the church, but that's as far as I got."

PI: "You've not been into the grounds behind it, where you've got the old Abbey, the walls, or the grounds there?"

SP: "No it looks spooky, so I won't go there."

PI: "You've never been?"

SP: "No."

PI: "In all the eight years that you've lived across the road from that park?"

SP: "No, that's all private so I wouldn't go there, it's a private area, it belongs to the church."

PI: "This is fairly open when you go past, would you agree with that or not?"

SP: "At the field yeah, the field is, but the church is behind the walls, I won't go past there."

PI: "Because three of the four people that have been found dead were found there. Slumped up against the wall near the Abbey."

SP: Softly mumbled "Yeah."

PI: "What was that?"

SP: "I didn't know that."

PI: "You didn't know that? So that's news to you, is it?"

Stephen then remained quiet, placed his hands folded together on his lap, and looked down at the map of the church on the table. What sounded like short sighs kept coming out of him as he started to rock back and forth.

PI: "Did you put them there?"

SP: "No."

PI: "You see Anthony (Walgate) was found outside of your address with a large amount of GHB in his system. The other three men we've been discussing were all found over by the wall area."

The detective then took his pen and started to circle the places that the bodies were found.

PI: "On the Abbey, you can see on this map again, they were slumped against the wall with a large amount of GHB in their body, can you account for that at all?"

SP: "No, I don't."

The detective then flipped the map over and brought out another page. The detective now had suicide note that was retrieved from the third victim Daniel Whitworth's hand.

PI: "Did you write this letter, here?"

The detective then pushed the page over towards Stephen.

SP: "No I did not."

PI: "This letter was found with Daniel (Whitworth)."

SP: "No."

PI: "Are you telling me the truth Stephen?"

SP: "I am telling you the truth, yes."

PI: "Now all of these boys, young boys, in the early stages of their youth really, in terms of their early twenties, all found dead, Stephen."

SP: "What do you want me to tell you?"

PI: "Close to your house. One of them had been in your house, either just before the time when he died, and was found to have large quantities of drugs in his system. The other three were found just over the road in the churchyard, or just beside the churchyard in the area that we've discussed, propped up against the wall, a short distance from your house, all again with high levels of GBH in them. Enough to kill them, highly unusual way to die for one person, this is four."

SP: "Right."

PI: "All found very close to where you live, all men, young me, the type of men that you say that you find attractive, all now dead Stephen."

Stephen remained very quiet, still with his hands in his lap, and looking downwards, not facing the detective.

SP: "As far as Anthony I know, the other three I don't know how they come to be."

PI: "Stephen this is serious okay?"

SP: "Yes I know."

PI: "It's really important that you tell us the absolute truth."

SP: "What I've said was true."

ANALYSIS OF STEPHEN PORT'S INTERROGATION

Stephen Port showed six signs of anxiety in police interviews that helped officers convict him of the four murders and several rapes.

1. Port would itch his nose,
2. Port had a very low volume in his voice, which indicated the words he was saying were not matched with the levels of confidence behind them. Port's body language showed constant signs of anxiety when the volume of his voice dropped with every answer. Dawn Archer, a professor of Linguistics, argued that there were indicators that Port was lying. *"Guilty speakers will use more negation, his volume drops, which suggest that the words he's saying aren't matched by a level of confidence. In other words, he's not believing what he's saying."* Experts also argue that it's a sign of anxiety when your volume is extremely low during the

interviews. When we are telling lies, we distance ourselves from our lies with our volume.
3. Port said "No" 40 times out of 47 questions asked by police.
4. Port kept closing his lips in order to make sure that he didn't say too much. He also kept crossing his arms in order to not leak information.
5. Port clenched his right fist and squeezed his hands. These were both signs of his body language showing his tension and that he was feeling under pressure. Later, as the questions got tougher for Port to answer, like when the interviewer asked Port if he was telling the truth about the boys, *"The type of men you say you find attractive, all dead now Stephen,"* Port replied in an almost inaudible low tone, *"apart from Anthony I know nothing about the other three or how they came to be."*
6. Port told the detective that everything he had told him up to this point was true. This is where Port squirmed his body around the chair, and clenched his hands. This indicated that he was hiding something.

6

TRIAL, CONVICTION, INQUEST AND APPEAL

The trial began on October 9, 2015, at what is called the Old Bailey, or the Central Criminal Court of England and Wales. Part of the prison stands on the site of the medieval Newgate Gaol, on a road named Old Bailey that follows the line of the city of London's fortified wall, which was also called Bailey. The actual court building on this property was built in 1902.

This crown court deals with major criminal cases from within the Greater London area. The trial that are held in the Old Bailey are open to the public, however they are subject to stringent security procedures. The first day that Stephen Port was brought into the court house, the grounds were full of screaming people, some of them crying and calling him names. Port just looked up at the Lady Justice statue on the top of the court building.

Placed around the wall of the entire hall are a series of references, some of them from the bible. Port would read parts of these phrases over and over while he was trying not to pay attention to any of the people yelling outside of the court house, and especially to keep from catching the eyes of one of the victim's family members.

"The law of the wise is a fountain of life."

"The welfare of the people is supreme."

"Right lives by law and law subsists by power."

"Poise the cause in justice's equal scales."

"Moses gave unto the people the laws of God."

"London shall have all its ancient rights."

| Gabriel Kovari

Prosecutor Jonathan Rees QC started out by telling the Court that Stephen Port would meet men through websites and phone apps such as one called *Grindr*, and that the case would feature graphic evidence of a sexual nature which they should approach in a cool dispassionate and analytical manner.

The prosecution argued,

"This is a case about a man, the defendant, who in the pursuit of nothing more than his own sexual gratification, variously drugged, sexually assaulted and in four cases killed the young gay men he had invited back to his flat.

Port described himself as 70% gayer than straight with a preference for young, smaller boyish type men often referred to as "Twinks." His appetite for penetrating drugged young men was reflected in the drug-rape pornography he watched, and he occasionally filmed himself having sexual intercourse with the unconscious males."

He had the propensity to render young gay men unconscious with drugs without their consent so he could have sex with them in that state. That was his inclination, his fetish, and what turned him on."

Rees then listed the drugs that Port had used on these young men as "Poppers or bottles of Amyl Nitrite, Viagra, M, also referred to as Meow Meow, T or Tina, the name for crystal Meth, and G, which was either GHB or GBL in its liquid form. GHB is of significance in this case. The post mortem examinations on the four young men who died revealed that each had died from a drug overdose featuring higher levels of GHB."

Rees finished with,

"Each of the victims were found outside, very close to Port's apartment, three of them in the St. Margaret's churchyard. The three victims found in the churchyard were propped up against the brick fence in the same position and with their shirts pulled up as if to have been dragged to their resting spots."

Rees then reminded the jury of Port's first arrest,

"It was after the death of Anthony Walgate, that Port was arrested and convicted for perverting the course of justice after he made false claims to the police. He had falsely denied ever having met Gabriel Kovari and Jack Taylor. Port also denied writing the false suicide note that was found in Daniel Whitworth's left hand."

Rees said,

"Port was a male escort, according to one of his former partners, Port described himself as having a big sexual appetite and who particularly liked men in their late teens. The defendant allegedly met with Walgate, a fashion student as a male escort, through the website *Sleepy Boys*, offering him £800 for an overnight, and met him at the Barking train station

TRIAL, CONVICTION, INQUEST AND APPEAL | 41

at 10 p.m. on 17 June 2014, using the name "Jo Dean." Walgate had sent a friend a text giving this friend full details of who he was meeting just in case he got killed."

Rees stopped and looked at the jury members one by one slowly before continuing,

---

"Around 30 hours later, at 4 a.m. on 19 June 2014, Port called the emergency services reporting that a young boy was collapsed or had had a seizure or was drunk on the street outside his flat. Port did not give his name and claimed that he was just driving by and saw the man. Police and ambulance attended, and a doctor pronounced Walgate dead shortly before 8 a.m., although its clear, he had been dead for some hours. The body contained a bottle containing GHB, and the postmortem revealed high levels of GHB in Walgate's blood and urine within the range at which deaths from GHB intoxication have been reported."

Rees continued his story, but now looking like he didn't believe what he was about to say,

---

"Port was discovered by police, who rung him back on his phone, asleep in his bed. Port then told the officers that he had found the man lying unconscious and had propped him up against the wall as he thought the boy had had a seizure, and then went into his flat and fell asleep."

The Court then heard about the eight victims who were still alive after they had been allegedly drugged and sexually assaulted by Port. The prosecution went on to say,

---

"It offends common sense to suggest that it was just an unfortunate coincidence that all of these men happened to either die or be sexually assaulted from an overdose featuring high levels of GHB, shortly after meeting with Stephen Port."

The first victim of Port's that the police could find was only 19 years-old, whom met Port in February of 2012 through the app Grindr, and was invited to his flat. The man claimed to have passed out and awoke to find Port having sex with him which he didn't consent to. The victim later reported to a counsellor that his drink had been spiked, and that he had been date-raped by Port. The victim also told some of his friends about the attack.

Rees then explained to the jury,

"There are similarities in these circumstances with the case of another man who, three weeks earlier, had been seen with Port at Barking station in a state of distress, and unsteady on his feet, incoherent, and vomiting."

Port had told the station ambulance and police he had found the 23-year-old under the influence outside of his home. The prosecution went on to explain that Port drugged him at his flat after the two men met through the website called *Fit Lads* by giving him a clear liquid, which he thought was water, and which caused him to fall unconscious.

When the man woke up, he found himself naked and lying on the floor. Port then helped him to get dressed and walked him to the Barking station. Rees said,

---

"He was deliberately drugged so the defendant could engage in sexual activity with him while he was unconscious. There is clearly a common factor underlying the explanation as to why each victim suffered an overdose, and that common factor is the defendant. The considerable efforts that he went to cover up his connection with each of the deceased indicates that it was he, rather than the deceased themselves, who was responsible for the fatal overdoses."

Rees went on to explain that Port took efforts to try and cover up his connections to each of his victims as well.

> "Each victim's mobile telephone was missing, and in each case, the defendant lied to the police about his knowledge of, and involvement with the deceased."

Port pleaded not guilty to the four murders, or the four counts of administering poison with the intent to endanger life or inflict grievous bodily harm, or the seven counts of rape.

On November 23, 2016, after the seven-week trial, Stephen Port 41, was convicted of the assaults by penetration, rape and murders of Anthony Walgate, 23, Gabriel Kovari, 22, Daniel Whitworth, 21, and Jack Taylor, 25, as well as the rapes of three other men he drugged, and ten counts of administering a substance with intent, and four sexual assaults.

He was found guilty on all counts.

Commenting on the case after the sentencing was Malcolm McHaffie, Deputy Chief Prosecutor for CPS London, said,

> "Over a period of three years the defendant committed a series of murders and serious sexual offenses against young men. Port manipulated and controlled these men through the chilling and calculated use of the drug GHB, which he administered without their permission. This was technically challenging case, complicated by a

significant amount of evidence taken from the numerous social media sites Port used.

The circumstances of each of the deaths were strikingly similar as each of the victims was aged between 21 and 25 and had died within a short time of meeting Port. Stephen Port had engaged in sexual activities with all of them, and they had died of toxicity from drugs, and in three cases a bottle of GHB was found in circumstances with being planted."

STEPHEN PORT APPEALS

On Thursday, August 30, 2018, Stephen Port, now 46, has lodged an appeal against his convictions for the murders of four young men, but not appealing the several other convictions of sexual offenses against seven other living victims. After lodging his appeal, a judge must now review the documentation that Port submitted to the court and decide whether to give the applicant permission to proceed.

Port was seeking legal advice to launch his appeal against the murder charges as he thought they were too high and untrue. Port figured that, if anything, he should have been convicted of manslaughter, since these deaths were a series of self-inflicted drug overdoses. He also claimed that it was proven in court that each of the victims had other drugs in their system including alcohol before they even met Port.

Another part of the claim stated that Port should have been more mature and assertive with the men when they were taking the GHB. Most people that know Port claim he is very young in the head, but no murderer.

The families of the victims spokeswoman immediately responded that it changed nothing and that Daniel Whitworth, 21, Anthony Walgate, 23, Gabriel Kovari, 22, and Jack Taylor, 25, were all drugged and raped by Port. After killing the men Port also tried to cover up his crimes by disposing of their mobile phones, lying to the police, and planting the fake suicide note on the body of the third victim.

On November 16, 2018, a judge dismissed Port's application to appeal at the first stage ruling out the need for his case to be heard by a panel of judges. Jack Taylor's sisters said that they were glad the appeal was dismissed because of the worry it caused them. It was quite a shock to them to find out that he had appealed the case in August.

INQUESTS OF THE DEATHS OF STEPHEN PORT'S VICTIMS

In October of 2018, it was decided that a judge would be appointed to conduct the inquest into all four of the deaths related to Stephen Port's conviction from 2016. It followed a request by the current coroner, Dr. Shirley Radcliffe, to allow the inquest to be held in a different area, or for her to step aside in favor of a judge. The results are expected to be in the hands of the victims' families sometime in 2019.

There has been a real public interest in the outcomes of these inquests, especially since the original 2015 inquest into the deaths of both Gabriel Kovari and Daniel Whitworth have been quashed. Those earlier open conclusions were reached when police had not connected the deaths of the four men.

The families of the victims were required to cover the legal costs of the inquests being held for their murdered family member. Jack Taylor's sister Donna told the *BBC* in September 2018,

> "We are trying to raise as much money as we can to have the best legal representation possible during the inquests because we think that, with what's happened, with the way we've been let down by the police, that we feel that we are going to need that."

But she thinks that its unjust that the police are assured of public funding for their legal representation, while the families are not. Donna said,

> "It's ridiculous after everything we've already had to go through, especially from our point of view to fight for this from the very beginning, to then find yourself in a position of having to do this now. It's just ridiculous. The boys were murdered, there's a huge amount of police failings, and under these circumstances it shouldn't be like this."

Mandy Pearson, Daniel Whitworth's stepmother agreed.

> "The police are dipping into public money. They can do it, no problem, and we've got to fight for what we need. A lot of this should be funded for us because, in the first place, the police didn't do their job. Otherwise Stephen Port would have gone to prison, we would have felt justice had prevailed, and we would have left it at that."

Mandy also thinks much bigger changes are needed.

> "There are so many families in our position that can't afford the legal costs and so there should be something there for bereaved families. We're not just fighting for us, we're fighting for changes in this law, where we should be funded, we're looking for changes all along the line."

The families applied for legal aid as well under the exceptional case funding scheme, but it's uncertain if they qualify for the assistance. The government revised the legal aid so that caseworkers consider when granting legal aid with the intention that funding would be more likely for those whose loved ones kill themselves or suffer an unnatural death while in custody of the state, such as in prison or a mental health unit.

The families were able to raise over 10,000 GBP from donations of over 300 people on a successful crowdfunding campaign on social media.

In another twist to the case, newly disclosed documents from August 2018, Stephen Port was awarded 135,383 GBP of taxpayer's money to cover his appeal to his four murder convictions. Considering the families of the victims were left to their own devices to raise money for their own costs surrounding the trial and legal fees.

7

FAILINGS OF LAW ENFORCEMENT

BBC *One* broadcasted a documentary in March 2017, that suggested a catalogue of police failings in the Metropolitan police's response to the deaths. Crucial witnesses were not questioned, such as Port's neighbor who had witnessed Port being in a dazed state, with a large container full of white powder and bottles of clear liquid, when he showed up unexpectedly to the neighbor's home. It was that same neighbor who claimed that he received weird text messages from Stephen Port about Gabriel Kovari.

After Gabriel Kovari was found dead, his previous room-mate, John Pape, did searches on the internet and was surprised to find several other unexplained overdose deaths in the Barking area. The cases had many similarities to the Kovari case. Pape found that especially in the Anthony Walgate case because their bodies were found in the same location. It seamed strange to Pape that the cases were not linked by the Barking Dagenham Police.

It wasn't until Daniel Whitworth was found dead in the

same park that John Pape called the police and demanded to know if the police thought the cases were connected and could be the result of murder. Pape was also very concerned for his own safety, but the police told him not only were the cases not linked, but there was no killer out on the loose to worry about.

John Pape then offered to come into the station to be interviewed by the police, just in case he had some relevant information about Kovari's death, as he knew about all the places and things that Kovari had done before his death, but the police showed no interest.

It was a very common belief in the neighborhood that the police had no idea what they were doing in not connecting the two cases. Barbara Denham, the dog walker that found the two bodies in the park even couldn't understand why they wouldn't link the two murders. Even the local gay organization, *The Pink News* was reporting that there was a serial killer in the area and to be aware.

On Friday May 12, 2017, the seventeen family members of the victims of Stephen Port filed a lawsuit against Scotland Yard, claiming that the officers discriminated against their relatives because they were gay. The High Court action is over "breaches of duty and inaction" and accuses the police of breaching the Equality Act 2010.

The families also claim that the police were negligent, and misusing or abusing their power by failing to properly investigate. Court documents revealed that they are seeking "aggravated and exemplary damages" in excess of £200,000.

The detectives admitted to missing the opportunity of spotting similarities between the killings.

It started when Port was jailed for the perverting the

course of justice in the death of Anthony Walgate, which ended up being his first victim. Port claimed that Walgate overdosed in his flat and said that he panicked and left the body out front of his apartment in June of 2014. He was only given an eight-month sentence.

Port then went on to kill three others after his release in September 2015. Some seventeen officers are facing misconduct probes after the case was referred to the Independent Police Complaints Commission. The families of the murdered men say they are insulted and distressed over the lack of police answers over the mistakes they made and why Port was not caught sooner.

Police then admitted catching Port due to missed opportunities and this leaves the families with new hope that there is an end in sight. The Commission had compiled over 7,000 pages of material on the cases and has their first draft completed.

It was during Port's trial that we found out that he was obsessed with pornography that focused on both men and women being raped while they were out of control on drugs. Port would go to dating websites or apps and meet up with his victims.

It wasn't until after Port's trial that the police introduced new guidance to deal with allegations involving "Chemsex" incidents. They must now review 58 cases where people died from GHB poisoning in London during the years that Port was active in the community. The police don't know the total as Port also drugged and raped seven other victims in separate incidents, where the victims didn't die.

Mary Person, Daniel Whitworth's step-mother said,

"We continue to seek answers and accountability from the police about how, for a whole year, they let us believe that Daniel had committed suicide, in which time Port went on to kill again. We really did hope that, with Port now behind bars, the police would be held to account for their activities. It won't bring any of the boys back, but we've been determined from the outset to get to the bottom of what happened and so we hope this will help with that. We wont rest until we get the truth."

FAMILIES OF THE VICTIMS FILE LAWSUIT

The families of the four men that were raped and murdered by serial killer Stephen Port are now suing Scotland Yard for more than 200,000 GBP. Claiming the police failed them, because the victims were gay.

Despite the striking similarities between each of the killings, the police failed to link them until the family of Port's fourth victim, Jack Taylor, forced a proper investigation of not only Jack's death, but the other three as well.

Jack's two sisters claimed that their concerns over the initial investigation went unheeded because Jack had been dismissed as a gay and druggie and that was it.

The papers filed on May 12, 2017 by seventeen of the surviving family members of the victims, state that the police breached their duties by inaction. They claim aggravated and exemplary damages from the police force because it breached the Equality Act 2010 by discriminating against the victims because they were gay.

Three of the claims read, "The Claimants estimate of the value of damages based on the current evidence is

50,000 GBP." Jack Taylor's family is suing for 60,000 GBP. Jack's sisters, Donna and Jenny Taylor said "The police should be held accountable for Jack's death. If they had done their job, Jack would still be here."

Immediately after these filings were made in court, the Metro Police issued their officers with a toolkit and checklist to provide guidance on how to respond to allegations involving Chemsex or party-and-play incidents.

A Scotland Yard spokeswoman said,

> "We are aware of a civil lawsuit action lodged in the High Court in connection with the Stephen Port case. It would be inappropriate to comment further at this stage."

Scotland Yard retired detective Colin Sutton, commented on the police department's handling of the case, and failure to link the killings for the *BBC* in November 2018.

> "I'm baffled to be honest. I can't explain how this could happen. Ultimately, all this stems from the fact that nobody recognized that these four very similar deaths of young gay men in a very small area were linked. They were treated as individual unexplained deaths rather than somebody looking as the bigger picture and the fact that they formed a series of murders all by one man. You've now got four deaths in the small area and of course the

connection's not that difficult to make because you've actually got a name, you've got Stephen Port who you know has told lies about the very first one."

A forensic psychologist Kerry Daynes, who is an advisor to the Home Office and to the Prison Service commented,

"I think the police failure in this case is literally catastrophic. Drug assisted sexual crime happens to members of all different types of communities and just because you're a member of the gay community, doesn't mean that you should be taken any less seriously than anybody else."

9

LETTERS TO CODY FROM PRISON

| Cody Lachey

PORT'S FIRST CONTACT

Shortly after Stephen Port's arrest, he received his first letter from Cody Lachey. In the letter, Port mentions that he has still not been allowed to see any of his family or friends and asks for some money from Cody for canteen goods.

Transcripts for the complete first letter **(unedited)**...

"Dear Cody, thank you so much for writing to me it's the first letter I have had since my arrest and I have not been allowed calls to my family and I have no idea how they are coping. I have written them a couple of letters and asked if they could top up my canteen money as I only have seven pound left after buying my essentials, coffee, biscuits, some white chocolate. The food here is alright but not enough. I was constantly hungry last week as after dinner at 4 p.m. there is nothing to eat until the following morning, and you only get a kid sized breakfast pack. If possible, could you send me an A4 writing pad and a pen in a sealed packet. (according to Cody that's for security) Please as this pen in running out already and I only got it on Friday.

Also, I know I'm being cheeky to ask but it gets so boring just watching TV in my cell most of the day. I would be very grateful if you could send me a magazine. I like 'Top Gear' films or 'Star Wars' but anything would be nice, hopefully some magazine will have a picture that I can put up on my wall.

I like Star Wars and feel sad I won't get to the new film next month. I will pay you back when I get access to my account. I have a single cell as I am a VP prisoner. (VP prisoners are vulnerable prisoners – the would probably be attacked if they were put into general population).

Everyone here has been alright with me, just the normal questions like did I do it or not etc. and I've been asked a few times to sign a picture of me in the paper which is the only article I have read describing me as a serial killer which is so ridiculous, as a serial killer has intent to kill, and you cant intentionally kill someone with GHB.

How would it even be possible to give someone a high amount without them knowing {it}, as it tastes vial. There's no way to disguise the taste, so the guy must know what he's taking and wants to be getting high on it. In the first place it has a slow effect, so some guys take more before its even kicked in and end up with a double hit.

However, some gays can take a large amount if they're used to it. My ex once drank a thirty-milliliter bottle full bottle of GHB when he was a wee bit high on M (methadone -) he was then rampant for a few hours, but then took some more M, and he was back to normal just with a sore throat as he didn't dilute it, so it burns his throat just a little bit. He was fine in the end. It's also quite addictive so wanting more is natural. If I wanted to kill someone, I would use an easier method like hitting over the head with a rolling pin.

I have been advised not to discuss my case with anyone as I am being monitored, but its common knowledge that I knew two of the guys. The first one I met online and when he came around, he took his own G (GHB). I wasn't watching how much he was taking as he seemed to know what he was doing and measuring his own dosage, but I am certain he was on other pills. Maybe prescription drugs which acted bad with the GHB, which mixed any system.

They didn't mention that in the papers, anyway I did call an ambulance when I saw he wasn't right, and I helped him outside to get some fresh air. He then sat down against the wall outside. I then saw the police arrive with an ambulance, so I panicked and went back inside.

A couple of hours later the police came and questioned me and said he was dead. I thought they were going to blame me and arrest me, so I lied and said I just saw him outside looking in and called an ambulance. But a few days later they arrested me as they checked his phone and saw that he had arranged to meet me.

So, I got charged with perverting the course of justice and I was sentenced to two months as a cut D prisoner in Brixton Prison, and two months on psych.

The other boy I met at a sex party I got invited to from Grinder. I can't remember too much about it due to the number of free drugs on offer out of the party. I did overdo it a bit and remember feeling sick. He and another guy asked where I lived and helped me home

I just fell onto my bed and passed out. I woke up after hearing a loud bang and a glass smash. I could also hear voices and shouting, but I couldn't move, I couldn't even turn my head. Its as if my body wasn't there, so I closed my eyes and slept until I woke up the following afternoon.

The flat was empty, just a broken glass, a spilt

drink on the coffee table. I cleaned up and thought no more of it. Please excuse my bad hand writing. I don't have my reading glasses. I have told the nurse and she said that she would make an appointment with the optician, but it could take three to four weeks and then it will be another couple of weeks to wait for the glasses to be made.

Why was you in prison? How long did you get? I was a head chef for a catering company but got dismissed when I was convicted (earlier for perverting the course of justice) back in March of 2015. I have been to Manchester a few times. I worked in Leeds for a short while a few years back and used to take day trips to Manchester with my boyfriend who lived in York. {Cody Lachey had told Stephen Port in his letter, that he lived in Manchester, and used to be in prison} My trial is not until April next year, so I have a long wait here. I do hope that you will write to me again, and I will answer more of your questions when certain you receive this letter, many thanks.

Stephen Port"

GETTING TO KNOW YOU

"Dear Cody, thank you so much for the money, I finally bought a pen and paper from the canteen. So, I can now write you many more letters. This is just a brief letter to let you know I received the money, so that you don't have to worry.

I will write a longer letter today and try and answer as many of your questions as I can. I have to write on your letters a number next to your questions 1,2, 3 etc. so I can look back and remember what you asked as I tend to ramble on and forget what you asked LOL.

They won't let me have the Star Wars Annual until I leave. So, I have asked my solicitor to write to the governor, so I have not shown any aggression towards anyone, and I have no history of violence of any kind. So, they have no reason not to give me the Star Wars book. But luckily, I got a Star Wars book from the library which had big print as I can see it as I have not got my glasses yet. Just there's no pictures in the book though. I can now order a Saturday Sunday newspaper thanks to your money, so I can have a TV guide, they sometimes have a magazine with it.

I won't yet order a 'Top Gera' magazine as I need the money to last, as I've spent 14 pounds already. I bought toothpaste, and imperial leather soap as the prison stuff is really crap. I got some coffee, digestives, caustic caramels, chocolate spread, porridge and some Jaffa cakes, which is no nice I ate them all at once, the whole packet on Saturday night while watching Doctor Who.

I have been watching 'I'm a celebrity get me out of here" I like George (George Shelley is all boy band pop music singer in the UK) and I'm certain that he will most likely win. Not just because he's cute, but he seems to be able to do any of the challenges that he's faced with.

I would love to come stay with you in Manchester when I get out of here, are you certain that would be okay? It's likely I will be allowed back to Barking, for my own safety, after what was said in the press. But I think I will sell the flat before I am released. Anyway, my friend Mike can take care of removing and storing my things, but I'm not allowed to contact him for three months. Ny sister is in contact with him though and says he's doing alright and living back with his family until he's allowed back to my flat.

He's been a good friend to me, we first met ten years ago when I was an escort. He was a client and we became really close as friends, not boyfriends as he was married with three kids. He helped me when I was in prison back in March. He looked after my flat and checked the post and paid the bills so that I still had a flat when I got released on an HDC tag. (you have probably noticed that Port contradicts himself by in one letter saying that he owned his flat and would sell it before he gets out, while in another letter his friend pays his bills for the flat as if he rents it)

He's going through a divorce, so I let him move into the flat as he wasn't happy in the family home. It helped me and it helped him. He gets on really well with my family and he became like a dad to my boyfriend, he didn't have parents as they disowned him for being gay, and he has autism. He used to help him with his college work and cook him dinner when I was at work, when I was doing a late shift, that was a few years ago though.

He got a job as a steward on the cruise liner and he's doing really well now, the ex-boyfriend, not Mike.

Being an escort is really dangerous, it's vital you never accept a drink from a client always take your own drink, take money first, and be alert. I had a friend who was also an escort and we would tell each other to where we were going and always gave the client's name and address or room number if it was a hotel. I would text him every hour to update him. He used to take some methadone before he went so that it made being with older men all the more bearable. But I preferred not to as I just wanted to get it done with, get paid and go home.

I never saw it as pleasure, just work which helped me save up a deposit for my flat. I only got into doing it when my friend said you're a good-looking lad with a nice body, why not make some money from it, and he told me what he did. At first, I was a bit nervous about having sex with all the guys for money. But it wasn't that bad most of the clients I had just wanted some company or to just touched me, some had the odd fetish and just wanted to dress me up in uniforms and take pictures of me etc. Some just paid me to go out for dinner with them. Would I be able to get a job on the doors or bar work in Manchester? As I want to get back into work as soon as possible when I am released.

To answer what I miss, I miss my home, my family and friends. Good food, DVD's, toys (Not sex toys Port actually liked to play with kid's toys) a comfortable sofa, going shopping and drinking, driving, and my last boyfriend and his beautiful smile, the way he kissed me, and would rest his head on my shoulder and kiss my neck. He had an amazing blue eyes and short ginger hair. He loved Minions and I used to buy him the toys. For his 23rd birthday I bought him a massive cuddly "King Bob' from the movie. I liked them a lot as they are so funny. I love the humor.

Are you dating anyone at the moment? I only started using Grindr when a friend and dealer had offered me free bags of methadone if I found him guys for his parties and to use my pictures etc. and I did a few times. And I never stayed long at his parties as he was into some heavy stuff I didn't get involved with.

I have a varying taste in music, I like the one by 'Nightwish', 'Adele', Will Young, I wished I could get his new album called 'Joy'. I heard it on CFL Friday's show.

Next letter to follow, all the best
Stephen Port"

SEND MONEY PLEASE

"Dear Cody, sorry for my rushed letters of the

weekend. I just wanted to let you know I received your letters and didn't want you to think I returned the items. I still don't know if they will let me have the Star Wars Annual, Cody had sent the Star Wars annual to Port after the first letter) well fingers crossed they will let me.

I know I can receive magazines if sent direct from W.H. Smith (U.K. Bookstore chain) but not certain about other items from suppliers. I was told that you could call the prison to find out, the numbers at the top of the page.

Not sure if they will allow me to have a watch or radio. I feel bad asking for cash, but if you could please post ten pounds, I can buy a pen, biscuits, order a magazine as hunger and boredom is getting me down. I will ask my dad to post the money back to you as soon as the bank will allow him access to my account.

I had asked the governor (Prison Warden) to write to my bank to give my dad full permission to access my bank account. He will have to cancel my direct debits like phone and internet, that will probably take a few weeks.

How was your weekend? What did you do? I hope I will be able to lessons or work soon so I can at least have some money on my canteen and get off the wing, as I'm feeling really really depressed at the moment. I'm just so glad I have you to write to, and I look forward to your reply.

I have a good legal team, and my QC is one of the best in the country. He's amazing and he's confident he can prove my innocents. I have told my parents not to speak to the press after all the lies, after they twisted everything to make it look certain I did it, when there's only evidence to link me to two of them. Which I mentioned before, but I would never harm anyone. I would sooner kill myself than take another's life.

I've been watching 'Big Bang theory' and glad there's new episodes on Thursday nights as seen all the repeats over and over. I don't follow my soaps but started to watch 'Neighbors' and 'Home & away' here. I also watch 'Star Gate' and 'Star Trek' when it's on. I can't wait for the new 'Top Gear' when Chris Evans takes over, but it won't be the same without Clarkson. But I love super cars so I'll be happy if I can get to see something like the new Aston Martin DB10, that's in the new Bond movie, wished I could see that.

Hopefully I will be out of here when the DVD comes out. So much more I want to write, but I have to give this pen back to the insider as its dinner time now and will get locked up after. I will post this on the way. All the best"

Stephen Port."

WISHED YOU WERE MY BOYFRIEND

"Dear Cody, just received your letter dated 19th of November. This week has been slightly better as I just started working in the ink shop, just filling up cartridges for printers but time goes fast. So, the day goes a bit quicker and the guys speak to me now and they don't seem to be bothered about why I am here.

They just take me at face value. One guy I've been working with said he thinks I'm a nice polite guy and said you don't seem like a murderer, and I told him I'm not and that I would sooner kill myself than take another's life.

Anyway, I only get two pounds, sixty a day Monday to Thursday, but at least it helps me buy essentials, but no luxuries though as just a pack of coffee is three-pound, ninety-nine and Jaffa cakes are pound. They're gone in one go as I love them LOL. I finally have an optician appointment for Monday.

So, I should have my glasses soon and my writing will become more readable, I hope. So, what have you been doing this week? I have lots of memories from my life, while being in here I remembered a lot of things I haven't thought about in ages.

My childhood was quite normal, my dad was strict but never abused me. My mum is quiet but speaks her mind when she wants to. I always had what I wanted within reason. At school I wasn't really bullied, but I used to get called stretch because I was tall and skinny, but at 16 I started going to the gym after reading some books on body building. After a few months my arms and shoulders started to get a bit bigger, so I didn't look like a bean pole anymore. I became better at sports and no one would bully me. (this is another contradiction as he just said he wasn't bullied, but when he worked out and became more muscular, nobody would bully him anymore?) I was quite shy, but I had plenty of friends as I was more of a jock, because I was good at basketball.

My ex-boyfriend was disowned when he came out as gay at 14, put into care by his foster parents, and sexually abused and ran away until he was put into the care of his granddad's, who was 76. He did his best but with him having autism and ADHD he was very difficult with his moods. He could become very aggressive.

However, at 18 he met me online and at first, he would just stay a week at a time. His grandfather used to drive him down, until I taught him to drive, and he got his own car. After 2 months he moved in with me for the first year we had a normal relationship with normal sex. I know you are probably thinking that I am the older guy, but I never had supply him with drink, and didn't know about drugs back then.

He was always horny and very loving, and we did everything together. He had his moods at times, and I had to call his grandfather to come down and help me as he would run out shouting and screaming in the street a few times. The neighbors would call the police, but it wasn't from anything I did, it could be from one of his friends online or I got a text from a friend that would upset him. He would get jealous very quickly, as he wanted my full attention, nobody else could have me. He didn't like change, everything would have to be as he wanted.

During the second year he met a friend online that was his age. It wasn't anything sexual between them, so I didn't worry. But he gave me methadone and said try it with Steven your boyfriend. So, we did it to give a try. It was amazing but after a while he would want me to try other stuff so his friend game him GHB. He was sick at first, but he kept wanting more, then after a while he started getting into the habit of taking GHB and being very submissive. He said do what you want to me I trust you. He wanted me to have control over him, and he wanted me to tie him to the bed.

Also, I can only guess as he was abused when he was young, that now it became a part of him. But instead of being forced to do it, he wanted it to be completely submissive. Sorry I am rambling again. I know you want to know more about me and not my ex-boyfriends, but he was such a big part of my life for four years, that was back in 2013.

When we split up, we didn't remain friends, but he didn't get on that well with my new boyfriend, they would clash and argue and they would both fight for my attention, so he went back to live with his grandfather and the new boyfriend moved in with me."

(On Cody's previous letter he told Port that he had been drugged sexually abused)

"Did you report this guy who drugged you? I could never do that because what's the point of sex if your both not enjoying it? I do prefer one on one sex rather than group sex, I liked his full attention and I want to give him mine. It's so much better with kissing and cuddling, also which you don't do in a group orgy, its just about getting in and coming etc. I prefer the real love.

I am being charge with administering a drug with intent to cause harm, which is murder times four. I was just charged with perverting the cause of justice as when my friend had a bad effect, I took him outside and left him there. When the police arrived and I said that I didn't know him, as I was scared. They then accused me of taking drugs with him. Now they accused me of giving him the drugs to intentionally kill him, which is so ridiculous. He was my friend and I would never do that, and I certainly didn't do that to my other friends.

It's most likely these guys had too much G, at a party and these guys took him to a park to avoid being done for drugs etc. or even maybe the guys enjoyed sex outside. I have done it in the past, it's quite exciting in the fresh air.

Anyway, I am not allowed to discuss my case as these letters could be used as evidence. But I have nothing to hide I have told the police everything I've just mentioned to you. My role models used to be Van Damme, Arnold Schwarzenegger and Chuck Norris and Sly Stallone. I took up martial arts and became a senior grade in Taekwondo-Do, I won five silvers in the British Nationals and a Bronze at the English Championships.

But as you've seen from my pics, I've never really gained big muscles just slim and toned because I had a really good six pack. I got a job as an underwear model for Jordan Conrad (British Fashion designer) Debenhams Range (high-end department store), and I used to have long blonde hair, so I looked like a surfer. I did swimwear too.

I'm just looking back at your letter and trying to answer as many of your questions as I can.

I like Doctor Who, I wish I had a Tardis LOL. (A fictional time machine or spacecraft in the Dr. Who series) I like the stories and adventures, Matt Smith was my favorite, but after watching a few episodes with the new guy, I think he's amazing? He fits the part as he looks older, it makes more sense as he's supposed to be 2000 years old.

I did like David Tenant though. I do like 'Family Guy' and 'Futurama' but the main cartoons I like are 'Transformers' and 'Marvel Avengers'.

I have been to Manchester's gay village, I was in a club there on New Year's Eve/New Year's Day back in 2007. I think I was with a boyfriend who lived in York. I was overseeing an opening of a restaurant in Leeds. I was helping train the staff and managers. I was living in a Travel Lodge (hotel) paid for by my company. I used to take the boyfriend out for dinner and charge it to the company, they never did know they were paying for two LOL.

I will get my canteen ordered tomorrow morning, more Jaffa cakes yummy. Thanks again for sending the 25 pounds, I won't say no if you want to send me more HeHeHe. I really do appreciate your loyalty and friendship, I wished you was my boyfriend. Can't wait to meet you when I get out of here.

Have a great weekend, best regards.

Stephen Port kiss kiss kiss."

PARTY N PLAY OR CHEMSEX

In the last decade with the development of networking apps created for the purpose of meeting others for the purpose of having sex, and the emergence of more drugs being cheap and available, a new type of gay sex called chemsex has come into the mainstream in larger cities like London.

The four main drugs used in chemsex are G.H.B, mephedrone, Alkyl Nitrites and crystal meth as they all have a sexual arousing property that the other mainstream drugs such as cocaine and ecstasy do not have. Users of these drugs can feel invulnerable to harm, very confident, lower inhibitions, sexually adventurous, a heightened sense of pleasure, and can possess a stamina and endurance that will keep them awake for several days.

The actual Party and Play or Chemsex is the consumption of these drugs to facilitate sexual activity and both terms refer to a subculture of recreational drug users who engage in high risk sexual activities usually in groups of several men. It is because the drugs inhibit ejaculation that the sexual encounters can continue for many hours.

The British Medical Journal released a report in 2015 warning that" chemsex needs to become a public health priority and even suggested there were deep psychological reasons why some gay men took part in it." The report goes on to say, "Some gay men were using these drugs to manage negative feelings, such as a lack of confidence and self-esteem, internalized homophobia, and stigma about their HIV status."

DRUG DEFINITIONS

- G.H.B. is short for Gamma-hydroxybutyric acid which is a drug known in the media as the 'Date Rape Drug" on the street it has several names that it known by including liquid x, liquid E, easy lay, natural sleep-500, scoop, fantasy, soap, cherry meth, g-riffic. G.H.B. mostly will come in a liquid form that is easily mixed with other liquids or drinks. It is a strong hypnotic depressant which can cause drowsiness, forgetfulness, seizures, slowed breathing, and slowed heartbeat. If a person was to take too much it could cause them to go into a coma which usually lasts two hours and another eight hours to properly recover.
- Mephedrone comes in either a powder or tablets and can be swallowed, injected, or snorted and produces erratic behavior, hallucinations, and delusions. It is quite often

taken with alcohol to increase the effect of the drug. Its street names are bath salts, drone, m-cat, white magic, and meow meow.

- Crystal Meth or methamphetamine is a recreational drug that stimulates the central nervous system and when used it can increase energy, lift one's mood, and increase sexual desire to such an extent that users are able to engage in sexual activity continuously for several days. It can appear as a crystalline powder or in a rock-like chunk, also known as ice, that vary in color between white, yellow, brown, or pink. It can be used by snorting, taken orally, injected or smoked. Methamphetamines common street names are Crank, Crystal, Crystal Meth, Christina, Tina, Cristy, Chalk, Ice, Speed, Ice Cream, Rocket Fuel and Scooby Snax. According to a documentary done by National Geographic on methamphetamine, the entire subculture known as the 'party and play' is based around sexual activity with methamphetamine use. The participants in this subculture consists almost entirely of homosexual male methamphetamine users, who will typically meet up through internet dating websites and have sex. Due to the strong stimulant and aphrodisiac effects during ejaculation, the participants will repeat its use several times. There is a crash after the use of methamphetamines can be severe enough to cause excessive daytime sleepiness.
- Alkyl Nitrites (poppers) are the names given to

drugs that are inhaled for recreational purposes, that typically give a 'high' or 'rush' and used quite often in the gay community during sexual encounters. Poppers have a relaxation effect on the involuntary smooth muscles, such as the throat, sphincter, and the anus. These drugs also cause an immediate increase in heart rate and blood flow through the body, producing a sensation of heat and excitement that usually only lasts for a couple of minutes. Poppers are usually taken through the nasal or oral cavity and in the UK are illegal so quite often they are packaged and sold as room deodorizers, leather polish, or tape head cleaner, to evade the law.

TIMELINE OF EVENTS

JUNE 4, 2014

Stephen Port is seen at Barking police station in the company of a young man who appeared unwell. Police were called but despite admitting taking drugs he could go.

JUNE 19, 2014

The body of Anthony Walgate is found slumped in the communal entrance to Stephen Port's flat in Barking. Port denies knowing him.

JUNE 26, 2014

Port is arrested after police discover he had hired Mr. Walgate as a male escort. He is charged with perverting the course of justice.

AUGUST 28, 2014

A woman walking her dog finds the body of Gabriel Kovari in the grounds of St Margaret's Church, a few hundred yards from Port's flat.

SEPTEMBER 20, 2014

The same dog walker finds the body of Daniel Whitworth in the same position in the churchyard. He is clutching a suicide note that turns out to have been written by Port.

MARCH 23, 2015

Port pleads guilty to perverting the course of justice in connection with the Anthony Walgate death and is jailed for eight months. He is released on an electronic tag on June 4.

SEPTEMBER 14, 2015

The body of Jack Taylor is discovered dumped in North Street, Barking close to Port's flat.

OCTOBER 15, 2015

Port is identified on CCTV meeting Mr. Taylor shortly before his death and is arrested on suspicion of murder.

NOVEMBER 2016

Port is jailed for life after he is found guilty of the murders of four young men - Anthony Walgate, 23; Gabriel Kovari, 22; Daniel Whitworth, 21; and 25-year-old Jack Taylor - using fatal doses of date rape drug GHB

ABOUT THE AUTHOR

Alan R Warren has written several Best-Selling True Crime books and has been one of the hosts and producer of the popular NBC news talk radio show 'House of Mystery' which reviews True Crime, History, Science, Religion, Paranormal Mysteries that we live with every day from a  darker, comedic and logical perspective and has interviewed guests such as Robert Kennedy Jr., F. Lee Bailey, Aphrodite Jones, Marcia Clark, Nancy Grace, Dan Abrams and Jesse Ventura. The show is based in Seattle on KKNW 1150 A.M. and syndicated on the NBC network throughout the United States including on KCAA 106.5 F.M. Los Angeles/Riverside/Palm Springs, as well in Utah, New Mexico, and Arizona.

ALSO BY ALAN R. WARREN

BEYOND SUSPICION: RUSSELL WILLIAMS: A CANADIAN SERIAL KILLER

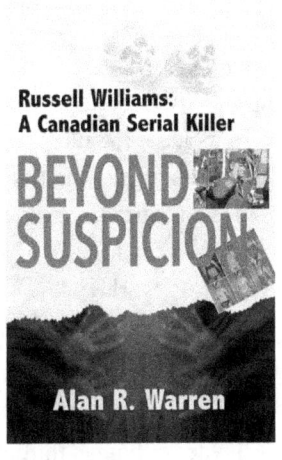

Young girl's panties started to go missing; sexual assaults began to occur, and then female bodies were found! Soon this quiet town of Tweed, Ontario, was in panic. What's even more shocking was when an upstanding resident stood accused of the assaults. This was not just any man, but a pillar of the community; a decorated military pilot who had flown Canadian Forces VIP aircraft for dignitaries such as the Queen of England, Prince Philip, the Governor General and Prime Minister of Canada.

This is the story of serial killer Russell Williams, the elite pilot of Canada's Air Force One, and the innocent victims he murdered. Unlike other serial killers, Williams seemed very unaffected about his crimes and leading two different lives.

Alan R. Warren describes the secret life including the abductions, rape and murders that were unleashed on an unsuspecting community. Included are letters written to the victims by Williams and descriptions of the assaults and rapes as seen on videos and photos taken by Williams during the attacks.

This updated version also contains the full brilliant police interrogation of Williams and his confession. Also, the twisted way the Williams planned to pin his crimes on his unsuspecting neighbor.

IN CHAINS: THE DANGEROUS WORLD OF HUMAN TRAFFICKING

Human trafficking is the trade of people for forced labor or sex. It also includes the illegal extraction of human organs and tissues. And it is an extremely ruthless and dangerous industry plaguing our world today.

Most believe human trafficking occurs in countries with no human rights legislation. This is a myth. All types of human trafficking are alive and well in most of the developed countries of the world like the United States, Canada, and the UK. It is estimated that $150 billion a year is generated in the forced labor industry alone. It is also believed that 21 million people are trapped in modern day slavery – exploited for sex, labor, or organs.

Most also believe since they live in a free country, there is built-in protection against such illegal practices. But for many, this is not the case. Traffickers tend to focus on the most vulnerable in our society, but trafficking can happen to anyone. You will see how easy it can happen in the stories included in *In Chains*.

REFERENCES

1. Khan, Shehab: *Stephen Port: Grindr serial killer appeals against murder convictions of four men,* Independent, Friday August 31, 2018.
2. Osborne, Samuel: *Stephen Port: Police investigate 58 date rape deaths after 'Grindr Serial Killer' found guilty of murder of four men,* Independent, Thursday November 24, 2016.
3. Osborne, Samuel: *Stephen Port Guilty: Grindr Serial Killer to be sentenced for murder of four men,* Independent, November 23, 2016.
4. Police interviews with GHB serial killer Stephen Port – London Scotland Yard – June 2014.
5. Metropolitan Police Service: *A man has been charged with four counts of murder in relation to the deaths of four men,* October 15, 2015.
6. Evans, Martin: *Gay serial killer Stephen Port*

guilty of date rape drug murders of four young men, telegraph.co.uk.

7. Kirk, Tristan: *Stephen Port murder trial: Gay chef murdered four men by injecting them with lethal doses of date rape drug*, London Evening Standard.

8. BBC News: *Stephen Port trial: Alleged serial killer 'tried to frame victim'*, October 6, 2016.

9. The Telegraph: *Families of men killed by serial killer Stephen Port 'insulted and distressed' over lack of police answers*, December 26, 2017.

10. Gayle, Damien; Davies, Caroline: *Alleged serial killer Stephen Port 'had appetite for sex with unconscious men'*, October 6, 2016, The Guardian.

11. Wilford, Greg: *Stephen Port: Police missed Grindr serial killer because victims were gay, families say in lawsuit,* The Independent. May 13, 2017.

12. The BMJ: 351 doi: https://doi.org/10.1136/bmj.h5790 (Published 03 November 2015).

www.ingramcontent.com/pod-product-compliance
Lightning Source LLC
Chambersburg PA
CBHW070939080526
44589CB00013B/1575